PREDATORS
GRIZZLY BEARS

Barbara Taylor

RAINTREE
STECK-VAUGHN
PUBLISHERS

A Harcourt Company

Austin   New York
www.raintreesteckvaughn.com

LOOK FOR THE PREDATOR

Look for the grizzly bear in boxes like this. Here you will find extra facts, stories, and other interesting information about grizzly bears.

Library of Congress Cataloging-in-Publication Data

Cataloging-in-publication data is available at the Library of Congress.

ISBN 0-7398-6600-1

Acknowledgments
The Publishers would like to thank the following for permission to reproduce photographs:
pp. 1, 5 (right), 7, 8, 18, 19 (top), 20–21, 29 John Shaw/Natural History Photo Library; pp. 2, 19 (bottom), 21 (top) Nina McKenna/Papilio; pp. 3, 6, 7, 9 (top), 9 (bottom), 14 (bottom), 17, 20 (top), 23 (bottom), 28 Andy Rouse/Natural History Photo Library; p. 4 Peter Cairns/Ecoscene; pp. 5 (left), 12, 23 (top), T. Kitchen & V. Hurst/Natural History Photo Library; p. 6 Robert Pickett/Papilio; pp. 10–11 Gunter Marx Photography/Corbis; pp. 10, 31 Corbis; pp. 11, 13 (bottom) George D. Lepp/Corbis; p. 13 (top) Lowell Georgia/Corbis Corporation Images; p. 14 Clive Druet/Papilio; pp. 14 (top), 24 (bottom), 25 Stephen Krasemann/Natural History Photo Library; pp. 15, 16–17 Ralph Kirchner/Natural History Photo Library; p. 16 Ralph A. Clevenger/Corbis; p. 22 Raymond Gehman/Corbis; p. 24 (top) Stuart Donachie/Ecoscene; p. 26 Joseph Sohm (ChromoSohm Inc.)/Corbis; p. 27 Roger Wood/Corbis
Cover photos: Natural History Photo Agency (DETAILS TO INSERT)

Printed in China/Hong Kong

07 06 05 04 03
10 9 8 7 6 5 4 3 2 1

CONTENTS

GRIZZLIES

Grizzly bears are one of the largest carnivores (meat eaters) on land. They are sometimes called "kings of the wilderness," because they are the most powerful predators, or hunters, in their environment. The only animals a grizzly is frightened of are humans . . . and other grizzlies.

HAIR-RAISING BEAR

The scientific name for the grizzly bear, *Ursus arctos horribilis,* means "the hair-raising bear." The first scientist to name the bear was so scared by its huge size and sharp teeth that it made his hair stand on end! So he chose the Latin word *horribilis,* meaning "makes one's hair stand on end" as one of the bear's names. *Ursus* means "bear" in Latin and *arctos* means "bear" in Greek, so the rest of the grizzly's name is "bear bear."

The grizzly bear is a type of brown bear that lives in North America. It belongs to a group of animals called mammals, which are covered in fur or hair and produce milk for their young. The tips of a grizzly's brown hairs may be grey, or grizzled, which is how it got its name. (Grizzled comes from the French word *gris,* meaning grey.)

The Eurasian brown bear lives in southern Europe and Asia. There were once brown bears living in the mountains of North Africa, but they all died out in the 1800s.

◀ The European brown bear is similar to (but usually smaller than) a North American grizzly. All bears have thick fur, a big head, small eyes, and rounded ears.

Black bears are North America's most common bear. They look like small brown bears but do not have a shoulder hump. There are ten times as many black bears as brown bears living in the forests of North America.

There are seven other kinds of bear alive today: the American black bear, the Asian black bear, the polar bear, the sun bear, the sloth bear, the spectacled bear, and the giant panda. All bears are very intelligent, curious animals with a good sense of smell. They can live a long time—up to 30 years in the wild and more than 44 years in captivity.

▶ Grizzly bears stand up on their back legs to sense their surroundings, to threaten an enemy, to reach for something, or to fight.

BIG BEARS

Can you imagine a bear that weighs eight times more than you do, whose head and shoulders tower over an adult human when it stands on its back legs? The biggest male Grizzly bears are this big.

Adult male grizzlies weigh from 285 to more than 800 pounds (130 to 365 kilograms). Male bears are usually 40 percent larger than females, which weigh anywhere from 200 to 500 pounds (90 to 230 kilograms) when full grown. Grizzlies are not the biggest brown bears, though. The biggest bear is another type of brown bear that lives on Kodiak Island, Alaska. Kodiak brown bears can weigh up to 1,600 pounds (750 kilograms)! Kamchatka brown bears from eastern Russia are almost as big.

ANCIENT GIANT

Millions of years ago, there were giant bears that were much bigger than Kodiak bears. The giant short-faced bear was twice the size of a Kodiak bear and the largest known carnivorous mammal ever to have lived on land. It probably hunted ancient camels, bison, and horses that once lived on the North American plains.

▼ Kodiak brown bears probably grow so big because they eat a lot of salmon, which is rich in body-building protein.

▶Although this massive grizzly looks fierce and frightening, grizzly bears mainly use their strength, claws, and teeth to defend themselves and to get food. They prefer to stay as far away from people as possible.

Size is not the only thing that makes brown bears such good predators. They also have a very powerful body, with short, strong legs and huge shoulders.

▼ The shoulder hump of a brown bear is made of fat and very strong muscles. The muscles give the front legs extra strength.

HOME RANGES

Most bears, including grizzlies, do not like other bears. They are independent animals that prefer to live on their own.

The only time you are likely to see more than one grizzly bear at the same time is when there is a lot of food, such as salmon, in one place, or when a mother grizzly is with her cubs. Each grizzly bear wanders over its own home range, which is a large area with plenty of different sources of food and places to rest. A home range may include a variety of habitats, such as forests, grasslands, mountain meadows, and river valleys.

▼Adult male grizzlies will fight other males that try to enter their home range and chase them away. Males will also fight during the mating season.

◀ Brown bears, such as the Kodiak bear from Alaska, spend most of their time traveling through their home ranges in search of food.

▼ Bears can only survive in remote areas away from people. This brown bear is climbing a fence in the Carpathian Mountains, Romania.

Because they are bigger bears, male grizzlies need more food than females so they have larger home ranges. They may wander over an area ranging from 10 to 400 square miles (25 to 1000 square kilometers) depending on how much food there is in the area. A female grizzly has a home area of between 5 to 77 square miles (14 to 200 square kilometers). It can be larger if she has to find food for her cubs, too.

HOMING INSTINCT

Grizzlies are very good at finding their way home. If they are captured by scientists and released outside their home range, it does not take them long to find their way back to their home range.

FINDING FOOD

Bears will eat just about anything, from roots, leaves, and berries to insects, mice, and deer. This makes them omnivores, which means they eat both plants and animals.

A grizzly bear's diet typically consists of less than 15 percent meat. Polar bears are the only bears that eat mainly meat, usually seals. Bears will also eat animals that have been killed by other predators or that have died from natural causes. If a grizzly cannot finish a meal all at one time, it will cover it loosely with branches or soil and go back to finish it later when it is hungry.

▼ A large grizzly can kill animals as big as elk, moose, or cattle, but they eat mostly small animals and plants.

What a grizzly eats depends on where it lives and on the time of year. In places where there are salmon in the rivers or on the coast, grizzlies are very good at fishing. During the summer in Yellowstone National Park, grizzlies climb high up the mountains to feast on army cutworm moths. They may eat 10,000 to 20,000 of these moths a day.

▲ Bears such as this black bear sometimes learn that our garbage dumps are an easy source of food.

▼ Grizzlies love the sweet taste of berries, such as buffaloberries, blueberries, and cranberries.

HONEY BEAR
Bears have a sweet tooth and will even swallow loads of angry bees to get at the yummy honey!

DEADLY WEAPONS

A grizzly's main weapons are its sharp teeth, long claws, and strong paws. Its jaws are also powerful enough to crack open the leg bones of animals such as elk or sheep to get at the juicy bone marrow inside.

▼ A grizzly bear may show off its sharp front teeth in a threatening display to scare off other bears or people.

GIANT CLAWS

A grizzly bear's claws are up to six inches (fifteen centimeters) long, although the front claws are almost twice as long as the back claws. They are useful for gripping and ripping open prey, digging up roots, opening up the burrows of small animals, and digging dens that they can sleep in during the winter. Sharp claws also help bears to grip bark when climbing trees.

▲ A park ranger shows the deep grooves scored in the bark of a tree by the huge claws of a grizzly.

Grizzly bears have 42 teeth. In the front of the mouth are long, pointed canine teeth for killing and holding prey. At the back of the mouth are broad, ridged molar teeth for crushing and grinding food.

A grizzly has five toes on each foot, with strong, curved claws for digging and tearing. The claws cannot be pulled in like the claws of a cat. On a grizzly bear's tracks, you can always see the claw marks ahead of the toe marks.

▼ A bear's long tongue is useful for licking up ants and honey.

SUPER SENSES

Grizzly bears rely a lot on their super sense of smell, but they also have excellent hearing. Their eyesight is about as good as a human's, and they can see in color, which helps them to recognize ripe fruits and nuts.

▶ Grizzlies can easily smell the food people leave out in their yards or campsites. This can lead to trouble if people and bears get too close to each other. If people come across a bear suddenly, the surprised bear may attack to defend itself.

◀ A grizzly bear has a long, pointed nose like that of a dog. It often raises its head and sniffs the air to check who or what is nearby.

Grizzlies can smell food from several miles away. They also use their sense of smell to find mates, identify cubs, and avoid people. By rubbing against trees, rocks, or the ground, grizzlies leave scent marks that tell other grizzlies, "I live here, so keep out!" Grizzlies also mark their home ranges with urine, droppings, and scratches on tree bark.

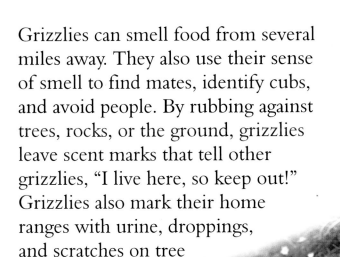

SMELL CHAMPION

The part of a bear's brain that detects scent is larger than in any other carnivore. Many scientists believe that grizzlies have a better sense of smell than any other North American animal.

▲ Using its senses of smell and hearing, this grizzly detects the burrow of a ground squirrel and moves in for the kill.

Bears are clever animals with large brains. They are very curious, learn quickly, and can remember good sources of food from year to year. But every bear is different and has its own personality.

GOING HUNTING

Grizzly bears spend most of their time either eating or looking for food. This is because they sleep through the winter and have to eat enough the rest of the year to make up for those months spent sleeping.

Grizzlies can hunt during the day or at night, although they are usually most active at dusk or dawn. Grizzlies usually hunt sick, injured, or baby animals rather than large, healthy adult ones.

▼ Grizzlies may rest in the middle of the day in day beds, which can be grassy areas or shallow holes in the ground.

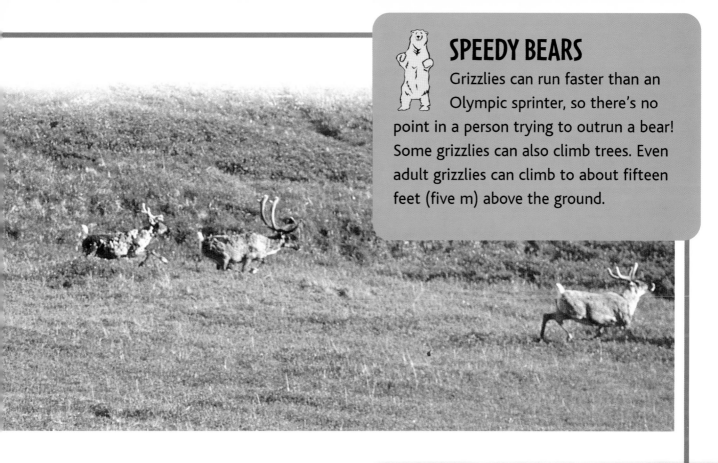

SPEEDY BEARS

Grizzlies can run faster than an Olympic sprinter, so there's no point in a person trying to outrun a bear! Some grizzlies can also climb trees. Even adult grizzlies can climb to about fifteen feet (five m) above the ground.

▲ With its strong shoulders and paws, a grizzly can knock a caribou (a kind of large deer) off its feet—if it manages to get close enough.

Despite their huge size and bulky bodies, grizzly bears can run at speeds of up to 35 miles per hour (58 kilometers per hour). This helps them to chase after prey, such as elk, moose, caribou, goats, sheep, and ground squirrels.

Adult grizzlies usually hunt alone, but several bears may chase after a herd of large animals. A mother grizzly will also hunt with her young cubs, teaching them how to track and kills animals until they are old enough to fend for themselves.

▲ Long, strong claws are useful when bears are digging for ants.

FISHING EXPERTS

Grizzly bears often gather to fish together when salmon migrate in from the ocean and swim up rivers to lay their eggs. There are thousands of salmon in the water at these times, and the bears have a real feast.

The salmon runs take place at different times of the year, but the grizzlies seem to know when the fish are coming. The most important time for the grizzlies to catch them is in the fall. They need the oily salmon flesh to help them build up stores of fat to survive the winter. An adult bear can eat 30 large fish a day.

LAZY BEARS

Biologists have seen more than 60 bears at one time in salmon rivers in Alaska. A group of bears is called a sloth. The word was first suggested in the Middle Ages when people thought bears were slow and lazy. (Sloth is another word for lazy.)

◄ The easiest place to catch salmon is at the top of waterfalls where the salmon leap out of the water.

▲ Salmon sometimes leap right into a bear's jaws. But they are very slippery, and the bear needs to keep a firm hold with its strong teeth and sharp claws.

▼ When food is plentiful, grizzlies will tolerate being near one another. But they will often fight over the best fishing spots, which usually belong to the largest males.

Different grizzlies have different fishing techniques. Some use the "wait and pounce" method. They sit on the edge of the river and wait for the salmon to swim past. Then they jump into the water, smashing the fish to the bottom of the river. Other bears stand in the middle of the river instead, and scoop out the fish with their enormous paws.

Once a grizzly catches a fish, it takes it to the shore. Using its front paws to pin down the wriggling fish, it strips the skin and flesh from the bones.

LEARNING TO KILL

Grizzly cubs are looked after by their mother and learn everything from her. Their father takes no part in their upbringing. Male grizzlies may even attack cubs and try to kill them.

A mother grizzly teaches her cubs how to find food, how to hunt, how to find shelter, and how to escape danger. The cubs watch her closely as she hunts and copy her techniques. In play fights, they practice combat by pushing and shoving, and trying to bite each other. Their survival depends on being strong and fearless. They learn these qualities from their mother and through play.

▲ Young bear cubs practice fighting to help them survive real fights when they are grown up.

▼It takes the cubs a long time to learn to fish as well as their mother.

CUB FACTS

Cubs are born between January and March, during the mother's winter sleep. The cubs nurse on her milk while she sleeps. She will occasionally wake up to clean them. Grizzlies usually have two cubs at a time and reproduce once every three to five years until they are about twenty years old.

Most grizzly mothers will have only four or five sets of cubs in a lifetime. They form deep bonds with their cubs and are very gentle and patient with them. They will defend them fiercely from any danger.

▲ Grizzly cubs stay with their mother for at least two years. Sometimes they stay with her for as long as four years before heading off to start a life of their own.

LONG WINTER SLEEP

Grizzly bears sleep through the winter because there is very little food for them to eat, not because of the cold. Their thick fur and layers of body fat keep them warm all winter. Grizzlies eat a lot of food in late summer and early autumn to fatten up for their winter sleep.

Some people call this winter sleep hibernation, from the Latin words for "winter home." Many biologists do not think that grizzlies truly hibernate. They call the winter sleep a dormant period, because the grizzly may wake up from time to time.

▼ A black bear cub in a den that it shares with its mother. The body heat of the bears keeps the den warm and snug all winter.

22

In the fall a grizzly makes or finds a safe, sheltered place, called a den, such as a hole in a hillside or on the bank of a lake or river. It will stay there for up to five or six months without eating, drinking, or getting rid of any waste. It survives by using nutrients from its layers of fat and by making its body slow down to save energy. Female grizzlies with cubs may lose 30 percent or more of their body weight over the winter.

▼ Only pregnant female polar bears and those with cubs live in dens in the winter. Other adult polar bears spend most of the winter on the ice, hunting for seals.

▲ When a grizzly cub wakes up from its winter sleep, the first thing it does is find some food to eat. Fresh grass and spring flowers taste good after long months with only its mother's milk.

WINTER SHUTDOWN

During its winter snooze, a grizzly bear breathes only three or four times a minute. Its heart rate also slows down from 40 or 50 beats a minute to about 8 or 10 beats a minute. Its body temperature does not change very much, though. It drops by only a few degrees, which means that dozing bears can easily wake up from their winter sleep.

UNDER THREAT

Grizzly bears once roamed over most of the western half of North America, from Alaska down to Mexico. Today they have disappeared from most of these places and are only found in large numbers in Alaska.

Grizzlies are threatened mainly by loss of habitat, hunting, and poaching for body parts, such as gall bladders, which are used in traditional Asian medicines. Some bears are used in circuses and other forms of entertainment. Other bears may be kept in terrible conditions in poor zoos.

▲ In some parts of the world, bears are shot for their thick fur, which can be sold to make clothing or rugs, or kept as a valuable trophy. Bear fur is usually a dark brown color but can be almost any shade between light cream and almost black.

◄ Bears that live too close to human areas can become a danger, and some of these bears have to be shot. Adult bears have short tempers and are easily irritated, especially if they are in pain. They are also very unpredictable.

► For their own safety, bears are sometimes moved to a new area. They may have to be moved many times because they often travel back to their old home.

Of the eight kinds of bear alive today, six are endangered, including grizzlies. Only polar bears and American black bears are off the endangered list, and even they would not survive without considerable protection.

To help bears survive, it is important to protect the places where they live and make sure they have enough space to stay away from people. Grizzlies are true wilderness animals that can only survive in relatively undisturbed areas.

HOW MANY GRIZZLIES?

There are now about 50,000 grizzlies living in Canada and Alaska, but less than 1,000 in the rest of North America. Alaska contains over 98 percent of the United States' population of grizzlies and more than 70 percent of the North American grizzly population.

25

BEAR FACTS

Here is a selection of interesting facts and figures about bears.

EARLY BEAR

The first bear appeared about 20 million years ago. It was called the dawn bear and was only as big as a fox. The dawn bear probably spent most of its time hunting in treetops. Much larger bears evolved from the dawn bear, including the European cave bear that roamed the Earth 50,000 years ago. It was about the size of today's Kodiak bears.

MYTHICAL CREATURES

For hundreds of years, bears have been the subject of legends and stories in many cultures. Most folklore describes the grizzly as a powerful, intelligent animal that people both fear and admire. Native Americans have many tales about grizzly bears raising children and healing people.

BROTHER BEAR

Native cultures often have other names for bears, such as "grandfather" or "brother" to show their respect for the powerful spirit of the bear. In

▲ A giant balloon in the shape of Paddington Bear, the lovable bear from the British children's stories. Other famous bears feature in well-known books such as *Winnie the Pooh* and Baloo in Rudyard Kipling's *The Jungle Book*.

Scandinavia, the Lapps of Lapland call bears "the old man with a fur coat," while the Finns of Finland refer to them as "the apple of the forest."

SPACE BEAR

In Greek mythology the Great Bear star constellation was said to have been made in the shape of a she-bear and placed in the heavens by Zeus. In Hindu mythology the Great Bear is worshiped as the power that keeps the heavens turning. The Eskimos believe these stars represent a bear being chased by dogs.

MAD WARRIORS

More than a 1,000 years ago, fierce Viking warriors called *berserkirs* were named after the bearskins that they wore. *Berserkirs* worked themselves up into a frenzy before battle. Today the word "berserk" means crazy or wild.

TOY BEARS

Teddy bears are named after President Theodore (Teddy) Roosevelt, who once refused to shoot a black bear cub on a hunting trip. Toy bears sold soon afterward were called "Teddy's bears."

NOSY TALE

Eskimo hunters share a widespread belief that polar bears will cover their black noses while lying in wait for a seal. But scientists have not seen this happen so far.

▼ For centuries bears have been chained up and forced to fight or dance in order to entertain people, as this ancient Roman mosaic shows. This isn't a pleasant life for any animal, especially an intelligent one.

BEAR WORDS

This glossary explains some of the words used in this book that you might not have seen before.

Bone marrow
A soft, fatty substance in the middle of bones that is rich in nutrients.

Canines
The large pointed teeth at the front of the mouth, used for killing and holding prey.

Carnivore
An animal that hunts and eats other animals; also known as a meat eater.

Den
A safe, sheltered place that bears sleep in during the winter.

Dormant period
The resting period when most of an animal's body shuts down to help it survive harsh times such as winters or droughts.

Grizzled
Spotted or streaked with white or grey.

Habitat
The place where an animal or a plant lives, such as a forest.

Hibernation
A dormant period during the winter when an animal's body processes slow down to save energy. The animal wakes up in the Spring.

Home range
The entire area that an animal lives in, including its home and the land that it roams over to find food.

Mammal
An animal with fur or hair. The females produces milk to feed their young.

◀ Sun bears use their long tongues to lap up insects and honey. They are the smallest bears of all and weigh only 145 pounds (65 kilograms). Sun bears live in the tropical forests of Southeast Asia.

Migration
A regular journey some animals make from one habitat to another because of changes in the weather or their food supply, or in order to breed.

Molar
A large tooth near the back of the mouth used to grind up food.

Native
The first people to have lived in a place.

Omnivore
An animal that eats all kinds of food, both plant and animal. Some bears are carnivores and others are omnivores.

Play fights
The pretend fights between young animals that prepare them for real adult fights.

Poaching
When people kill or capture animals illegally.

Predator
An animal that hunts other animals and eats them.

Prey
An animal that is hunted and killed by another animal (a predator).

Protein
A type of food that animals need for growth and repair of their bodies.

Reproduce
The process of producing young.

Urine
A liquid made with the body's waste water and chemicals.

▶ Grizzlies are usually quiet animals but they will often grunt, growl, or even roar to communicate or to frighten other bears and people away.

BEAR PROJECTS

If you want to find out more about bears, here are some ideas for projects.

WATCHING BEARS

You may be able to visit a zoo or a park that bears are known to live in. Watch the bears carefully to see how they move, feed, and interact with people or other animals.

BEAR SAFETY

If you are lucky enough to be able to visit places where wild bears live, here are some rules to remember so you will not to disturb them or make them angry.

● Before going camping or hiking, always ask park rangers if there are bears in the area.

● Try not to surprise bears. Make a noise, such as clapping hands, singing, ringing bells, or shaking stones in a can. This warns any bears you are coming so they can get out of the way.

● Store food and garbage in bear-proof containers or keep it high up—well out of reach of bears.

If you do meet a bear, freeze.

● Try not to stare at the bear and slowly back away if the bear ignores you. If the bear approaches, curl up in a ball and cover your head. Do not run.

● Never get between a mother and her cubs.

● Stay away from dead animals. A bear may be returning to feed later and might think you are trying to steal its food.

BEARS AND HONEY

Bears are well known for their love of honey and other sweet foods. Look for bears on food labels in supermarkets and in advertisements in magazines or on television. Make a list of the products associated with bears. How do these relate to the way bears live in the wild?

HOW YOU CAN HELP

Join a conservation group to find out more about bears and see how you can help bears survive in the future. You may be able to "adopt" a bear and help to pay for its upkeep. Here's the address of one conservation group:

Bear Trust International
P.O.Box 4006,
Missoula, Montana 59806-4006
Email: inquiry@beartrust.org

National Wildlife Federation
www.nwf.org/grizzly/index.cfm
Legends and facts about hiking in grizzly country.

Canadian Wildlife Service
www.cws-scf.ec.gc.ca/hww-fap/grizzly/
      grizzly.html
Lots of information about grizzly distribution, physical characteristics, life history, food habits, home ranges, and relationship to people.

BEARS ON THE WEB

If you have access to the Internet, try looking up these websites:

Bear Trust International
www.beartrust.org
Information about grizzlies and other bears, plus bear facts, bear news, and details of bear conservation and how you can volunteer to help protect wild bears.

North American Bear Center
www.bear.org
A great site with lots of detail about grizzlies and other bears, including slide shows, a typical day of grizzly watching, and a kids' area with different bear sounds.

▼ **Grizzly bears are considered to be threatened in the United States and vulnerable in Canada. It will be tragic if we cannot find a way of sharing the wilderness with these magnificent animals.**

INDEX